Molecules and Atoms

by Edward Victor

ILLUSTRATED BY JOHN HULL

Follett Publishing Company   Chicago • New York

Library of Congress Catalog Card Number: 63-9623

THIRD PRINTING   TLA 5860

Did you know that everything around you
is made of very tiny bits or particles?   These
bits are so tiny that you cannot see them with
your eyes.

Scientists call these tiny bits molecules.

Molecules are so tiny that a teaspoon of water has many billions of molecules in it.

The food you eat, the milk you drink, and the air you breathe are all made of molecules.

The clothes you wear, the furniture you use, and the toys you play with are all made of molecules. You are made of molecules!

You cannot see the molecules, but they are there.

5

Wood (solid)   Water (liquid)   Air (gas)

These tiny molecules, or bits of matter, are always moving.

In a gas such as air, the molecules move around very freely and very quickly.

In liquid matter, like water or milk, the molecules move around quickly but stay close to each other.

In solid matter, like wood or metal, the molecules do not move very far, but shake quickly back and forth.

All matter is either a solid, a liquid, or a gas.   These are the three states of matter that scientists talk about.

In a solid or a liquid the molecules are very close together. In a gas the molecules are much farther apart than they are in a solid or a liquid.

You can do an experiment to show there are spaces between molecules. Get a glass of water. Put a spoonful of salt in the water. Stir the water with the spoon until the salt disappears.

Where did the molecules of salt go? They all went into the spaces between the molecules of water.

If we know about molecules, we can explain many things around us. We can understand what heat is.

Scientists tell us that when molecules move faster, things get hotter. When the molecules move slower, things get cooler.

We can make molecules move faster by giving them more energy. We can make molecules move slower by taking energy away from them.

The fast-moving balls are something like the fast-moving molecules in hot water.

A hot stove gives off heat energy. This energy passes into the water and makes the molecules of water move faster. And so the water gets hotter.

If we put a piece of ice into the water, heat energy passes from the hot water molecules to the cold ice molecules. The water gets cooler and the ice gets warmer.

The slower-bouncing balls are something like the slower molecules in cooling water.

Heat can turn solids into liquids.   It can turn liquids into gases.   This is called changing the state of matter.

Ice is a solid.   Solids have their own size and shape.   If solid ice is heated, the molecules begin to move faster.   The ice gets warmer.   Soon it turns into water, or melts.

Water is a liquid.   Liquids have size, but do not have a shape of their own.   They take the shape of whatever holds them.   But when a liquid changes its shape, this does not mean that we suddenly have more liquid or less liquid.   We still have just as much.

When water boils, bubbles of gas appear. The gas is invisible water vapor. Like other gases, water vapor has no size or shape of its own. Its molecules move freely. Vapor rises in boiling water because it is lighter than water. The bubbles pop and the water vapor goes into the air. Some of it turns back into tiny drops of liquid that we can see as a cloud. Some of the invisible water vapor just mixes with the air molecules in the room.

Other kinds of matter can be changed from a solid into a liquid into a gas. The state of iron and other metals can be changed this way.

It is important to remember that the molecules of ice, liquid water, and water vapor are all of the same kind. Only the state of the matter is different, because the molecules have different amounts of energy.

The pan in the picture on the left has water in it. The picture on the right shows the same pan days later. The water has all disappeared. This happens because the molecules on top of the water, which are moving, can sometimes "jump" into the air even without being heated. This is called evaporation. Solids can evaporate, too. When you smell a moth ball, you smell some of its molecules that have turned into a gas.

Liquids and solids will evaporate, or turn to a gas, if their molecules have enough energy.   Giving molecules more energy—by heating them—makes it easier for the liquids and solids to evaporate.

If energy is taken away from gas molecules they condense.   This means that they come closer and closer together and turn into a liquid when they lose enough energy.   Water vapor condenses easily.   The drops of water that appear on the outside of cold things have condensed from water vapor in the air.

Air molecules condense and turn to a liquid, too.   But this happens only at very, very low temperatures.

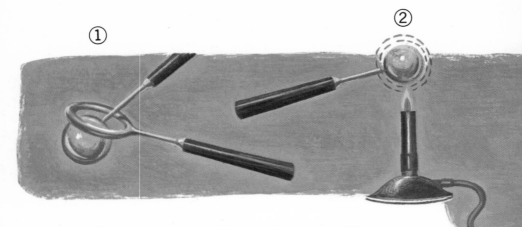

When we heat things, they get bigger, or expand. When we cool them, they get smaller, or contract. The movement of molecules explains why this happens.

In the picture on this page there is a metal ball and a metal ring. The ball can pass through the ring. (Picture #1)

When we heat the ball, it gets bigger, or expands. (Picture #2) What happens is that the molecules move faster. The molecules move farther apart and take up more space. When they take up more space, the ball gets bigger, or expands.

Now the ball cannot pass through the ring. It is too big. (Picture #3)

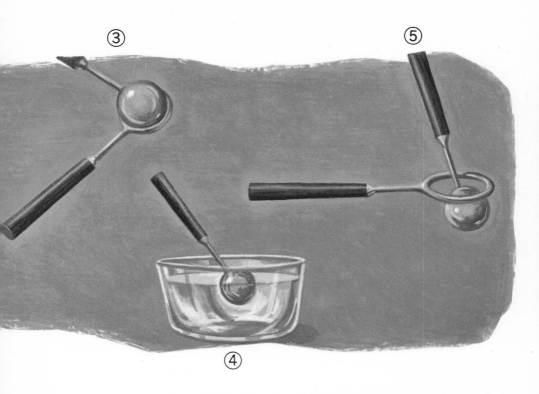

③ ⑤

④

When we cool the ball, the molecules in the ball move more slowly. (Picture #4) They come closer together and take up less space.

The ball becomes smaller, or contracts. Now it can go through the ring again. (Picture #5)

In just the same way, liquids will expand when they are heated and contract when they are cooled.

And the same thing happens to gases.

The movement of molecules helps heat to travel. If you heat a metal rod at one end the molecules at that end begin to move faster. The faster moving molecules bump into other molecules next to them and make these molecules move faster too.

This goes on and on. Molecules keep bumping into more molecules. Soon all the molecules in the metal rod are moving faster.

In this way the rod gets hot from one end to the other end.

This kind of heat travel is called conduction. It works best with solids like metals, where the molecules are very close together.

The movement of molecules helps sound
to travel, too. When a bell rings, first the
clapper hits the bell. The bell moves back
and forth very fast, or vibrates.

The vibrating bell hits the molecules of
air around it and makes them vibrate.

The molecules then bump into other
molecules and start them vibrating.

This goes on and on. Molecules keep
bumping into other molecules. Soon they all
begin to vibrate. So the sound of the bell
is carried from molecule to molecule.

This is the way molecules help sound
travel through gases, liquids, and solids.

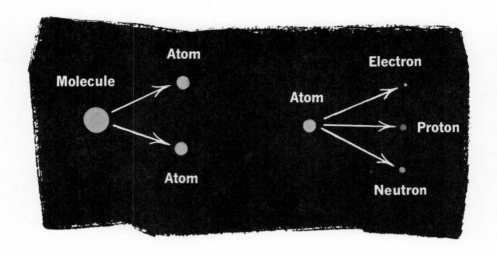

Molecules are very small particles. But they are not the smallest bits of matter we know. Molecules are made of even smaller particles called atoms. Some molecules, such as iron, have only one atom. The molecule of "heavy hydrogen," shown in the picture above, has two atoms of the same kind.

Atoms can be separated into still smaller particles. The most important of these smaller particles are the proton, the neutron, and the electron.

18

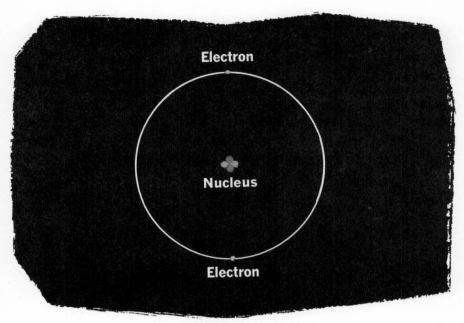

An atom of helium

There are many, many different kinds of atoms. They all have different sizes. But they are all put together in much the same way.

The center of the atom is called the nucleus. The protons and neutrons of the atom are in the nucleus. Outside the nucleus are the electrons. They whirl around the nucleus.

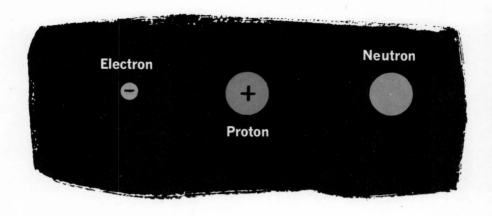

Protons and neutrons have just about the same size and weight. But electrons weigh much less than protons or neutrons.

Scientists tell us that electrons and protons have electricity in them. There are two kinds of electricity, negative (−) and positive (+). The electrons are said to have a negative electrical charge. The protons are said to have a positive electrical charge.

Neutrons do not have a positive or a negative electrical charge.

The simplest atom is the hydrogen atom. Its nucleus has just one proton. One electron whirls around this nucleus. Another kind of hydrogen is called "heavy hydrogen." It also has only one electron, but its nucleus has one proton and one neutron. Page 19 shows a helium atom. Its nucleus has two protons and two neutrons. Two electrons whirl around it.

Hydrogen atom

Electron

+ Proton

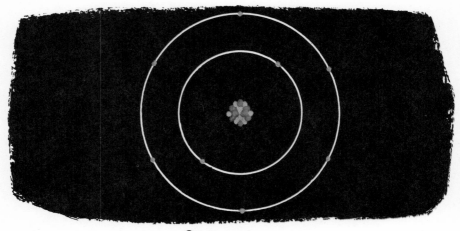

Oxygen atom

The picture above shows a larger kind of
atom.   It is an oxygen atom found in the air.
Oxygen has eight protons and eight electrons.
There are also eight neutrons inside the nucleus.
On page 21 you read about two kinds of hydrogen.
And there are different kinds of oxygen, too.
One kind of "heavy oxygen" has nine neutrons.
Another kind has ten neutrons.   But all of these
kinds have only eight protons and eight electrons.

Atoms that have the same number of protons
and electrons, but different numbers of neutrons,
are called isotopes.

Uranium-235 atom

The uranium atom is one of the heaviest kinds. There are at least 14 different kinds of uranium isotopes. They all have 92 protons and 92 electrons, but their number of neutrons is not the same.

The number of electrons and protons in one kind of atom is usually the same. Scientists call the number of protons the "atomic number." All atoms with an atomic number of 1 are hydrogen. All atoms with an atomic number of 8 are oxygen. All atoms with an atomic number of 92 are uranium.

23

The different kinds of atoms are called elements. Element number one is hydrogen. It has a name as well as a number. Each of the other elements has a name, too. When scientists write about elements, they sometimes write the names in a short way. When the name is written in a short way, it is called a symbol. The chart below shows some of the symbols of common elements. There are more than 100 different elements. Most of them have several isotopes.

Some common elements and their symbols

Hydrogen	H	Silicon	Si	Silver	Ag
Helium	He	Sulfur	S	Tin	Sn
Carbon	C	Chlorine	Cl	Iodine	I
Nitrogen	N	Calcium	Ca	Gold	Au
Oxygen	O	Iron	Fe	Mercury	Hg
Neon	Ne	Nickel	Ni	Lead	Pb
Sodium	Na	Copper	Cu	Radium	Ra
Aluminum	Al	Zinc	Zn	Uranium	U

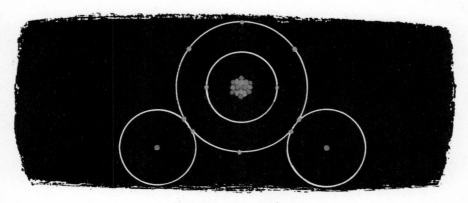

A molecule of water

Elements are like building blocks. Atoms of different elements can be put together to make different molecules.

Let's take a look at a molecule of water. It is made of three atoms. It has two atoms of hydrogen and one atom of oxygen. Together all three atoms make one molecule of water.

Scientists use the symbols for hydrogen and oxygen when they write the name for water. They write it H_2O.

You can see that this means two atoms of hydrogen put together with one atom of oxygen. Scientists call H_2O a formula for water.

Salt is made of two atoms. It has one atom of the element sodium and one atom of the element chlorine. Using the symbols for sodium and chlorine, the formula for salt is NaCl.

Sugar is made of 45 atoms. It has 12 atoms of the element carbon, 22 atoms of the element hydrogen, and 11 atoms of the element oxygen. Its formula is $C_{12}H_{22}O_{11}$.

The formula shows what kinds of atoms a molecule has, and also how many of each.

Salt and sugar look alike. But they are made of different atoms.

Electrons flow from a dry cell through the
copper wire in the cord to the light bulb
and back to the dry cell.

Knowing about atoms and their particles
helps us understand many things. It helps us
understand what electricity is.

In some elements the electrons can leave
the atom very easily and move about freely.
This happens best with elements that are metals.

Electricity is the movement of these free
electrons through the metals.

This is why metals are used to carry, or
conduct, electricity. The copper metal in your
electric cords is used to conduct electricity.

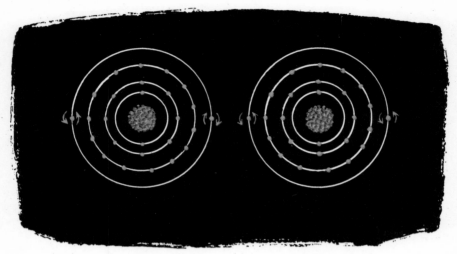

Outside electrons spinning
in different directions

Outside electrons spinning
in the same direction

Knowing about atoms helps us understand why we have magnets.

In all of the elements the electrons spin like a top as they whirl around the nucleus of the atom. For most elements about half of the electrons in each atom spin in one direction, and half spin in the other direction.

In some elements, like iron, there are more electrons spinning in one direction than in the other direction. These elements can become magnets.

Atomic plant for producing electricity   Submarine run by atomic power

Scientists have learned very much about molecules and atoms. They can take molecules apart and put the atoms back together in different ways to make different things.

They have taken the atom apart. They have learned to use the energy from the atom to run submarines and ships.

There is still much to learn. We do not understand exactly how the particles stay together in the atom. We do not understand exactly how atoms make molecules.

But every day scientists are learning more about molecules and atoms.

Words Younger Childen May Need Help With

(Numbers refer to page on which the word first appears.)

4	particles	18	atoms		nitrogen
	molecules		hydrogen		neon
5	teaspoon		proton		sodium
	furniture		neutron		aluminum
7	experiment		electron		silicon
8	energy	19	nucleus		sulfur
11	vapor	20	electricity		chlorine
	invisible		negative		calcium
12	evaporation		positive		iodine
13	condense	21	helium		mercury
	temperatures	22	oxygen		radium
14	expand		isotopes	25	formula
	contract	23	uranium	27	conduct
16	conduction	24	elements	28	magnets
17	vibrate		symbol	29	submarine

THINGS TO DO IN THE CLASSROOM OR AT HOME

Fill a glass with cold water. Put a few drops of red food coloring into the water. See how long it will take for the red coloring to spread out all through the water. The water will turn the same red color even without stirring. This happens because the molecules of water are moving. These moving molecules push the molecules of red coloring around until the water has the same red color everywhere.

Now do this experiment again, but this time use a glass of warm or hot water. Make sure that there is just as much hot water in the second glass as there was cold water in the first glass. Also, put the same number of drops of red coloring in the second glass as you did in the first glass. See how much more quickly the hot water becomes red all over. In hot water the molecules of water move faster than in cold water. The faster moving molecules push the molecules of red coloring around more quickly.

Put a lump of sugar in a glass of cold water. Stir the water until the sugar disappears. When this happens, we say that the sugar dissolves in the water. The molecules of sugar go into the spaces between the molecules of water. Put more sugar into the water, one lump at a time, and stir the water after you put in each lump, until no more sugar will dissolve. When this happens, all the spaces between the molecules of water are filled with molecules of sugar.

Now do this experiment again, but this time use a glass of warm or hot water. More sugar will dissolve in the hot water. When water is hot, its molecules move faster and farther apart. This makes the spaces between the molecules become bigger. There is now more room in these spaces for more molecules of sugar. So, more sugar will dissolve in hot water than in cold water.

Make a display of elements. You will find a list of all the elements we know in a chemistry book or in an encyclopedia. You should be able to find copper, silver, gold, iron, lead, mercury, tin, and many other elements.

Get a thermometer that has colored liquid inside it. See for yourself that liquids will expand when they are heated and will contract when they are cooled. Put your finger on the glass bulb at the bottom of the thermometer. The heat from your finger will make the liquid expand and move higher up the glass tube. When you take your finger away, the liquid becomes cooler. Now the liquid will contract and become smaller, and the liquid will move down the glass tube.

Make a long row of dominoes. Stand them all up on one end. Keep each domino about one inch away from the next domino. Now push the domino at one end and make it fall against the domino next to it. All the dominoes will fall down, as each one hits the other. This will give you some idea of how vibrating molecules can make other molecules vibrate too.

Make picture models on paper of some of the atoms. Draw some circles, with one circle inside the other. Tack or paste the paper to some thick cardboard or to the bulletin board. Now get some thumbtacks with colored heads. Use three different-colored tacks. One color will stand for protons, the second color for neutrons, and the third color for electrons. Use a chemistry book or an encyclopedia to find out just how many protons, electrons, and neutrons there are in the atoms you picked for models. Use the smallest circle for the nucleus. In the nucleus put in enough colored tacks to give you the right number of protons and neutrons that belong there. In the other circles put in the right number of colored tacks, or electrons, for each circle. Now write the name of the element on each piece of paper and put the chemical symbol beside the name. Then list the number of protons, electrons, and neutrons that belong to the atom. Also, tell which colored tack stands for the proton, the electron, and the neutron.